The gingerbread man

Story written by Gill Munton
Illustrated by Tim Archbold

Speed Sounds

Consonants   *Ask children to say the sounds.*

f ff ph	l ll le	m mm mb	n (nn) kn	r (rr) wr	s ss se ce	v ve	z zz se s	sh	th	ng (nk)

b bb	c k ck	d dd	g gg	h	j g ge	p pp	qu	t tt	w wh	x	y	ch (tch)

Each box contains one sound but sometimes more than one grapheme.
*Focus graphemes for this story are **circled**.*

4

Vowels

Ask children to say the sounds in and out of order.

a	e / ea	i	o	u	ay	ee / y	igh / i	ow / o
at	hen	in	on	up	day	see	high	blow

oo	oo	ar	or / oor / ore	air	ir	ou	oy / oi
zoo	look	car	for	fair	whirl	shout	boy

Story Green Words

Ask children to read the words first in Fred Talk and then say the word.

test   fresh   crisp   cloth   felt like lead

Ask children to say the syllables and then read the whole word.

curr|ants   butt|ons   craft|y   dust|y   o|ven*   ging|er|bread*

Ask children to read the root first and then the whole word with the suffix.

finish → finished   wink → winked   pull → pulled

sniff → sniffed   lift → lifted   stick → sticky   gasp → gasped

grin → grinned   lick → licked

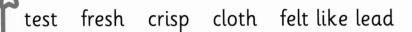

* Challenge Words

6

Vocabulary Check

Discuss the meaning (as used in the story) after the children have read each word.

	definition:	**sentence:**
currants	small black fruit like raisins	Ann put down the bag of currants.
gasped	breathed heavily, out of breath	"Stop!" gasped Seth.
felt like lead	really heavy	They ran so fast that their legs felt like lead.
crafty	clever	Then the crafty old fox began to run.
dusty	dirty, dry mud	The fox led him along a dusty track.

Red Words

Ask children to practise reading the words across the rows, down the columns and in and out of order clearly and quickly.

to	was	her	said
you	you	of	was
they	their	was	want
some	small	all	are
were	do	school	what

The gingerbread man

Hands, legs, a head ...

Six currants for buttons ...

and the last gingerbread man was finished!

Ann put down the bag of currants.
Her husband Seth pushed the tin of
gingerbread men into the hot oven.
That was when the last gingerbread man ... winked!

"I think I will get them out of the oven,"
said Seth at six o'clock.

He pulled the tin out, sniffed,
and bit off a bit of leg.

"Well, I have got to test them," he said.
"Mmmm! Fresh and crisp! Not bad!"

He left the tin next to the bread bin,
with a cloth spread on top.

The last gingerbread man lifted his sticky head
off the bottom of the tin.
He lifted the cloth. He lifted his legs – and jumped out!
He ran out of the kitchen!

"Stop!" yelled Seth.
"Stop!" yelled Ann.
He ran from Seth and Ann, singing,
"Run, run, as fast as you can!
You can't catch me.
I am the gingerbread man!"

Ann's black cat Lucky began
to run as well.

"Stop!" yelled Seth.
"Stop!" yelled Ann.
"Stop!" yelled Lucky.
But the gingerbread man ran on.

"Run, run, as fast as you can!
You can't catch me. I am the gingerbread man!"

Seth's fat dog Bonzo began to run as well.
"Stop!" gasped Seth. "Stop!" gasped Ann.
"Stop!" gasped Lucky. "Stop!" gasped Bonzo.
They ran so fast that their legs felt like lead.
They had to stop to rest.

But the gingerbread man ran on.
"Run, run, as fast as you can!
You can't catch me.
I am the gingerbread man!"

Then the crafty old fox began to run.

"Stop!" he yelled. "Let me help you, gingerbread man!"

He licked his lips.

The gingerbread man stopped running
and grinned at the crafty old fox.

"Well, thanks!" he said.

The fox led him along a dusty track.
At the end of it was his den.
The crafty old fox licked his lips ...
and that was the end of the gingerbread man!

Questions to talk about

Ask children to TTYP each question using 'Fastest finger' (FF) or 'Have a think' (HaT).

p.9 (FF) What did the gingerbread man do as he was put in the oven?

p.10 (FF) How did Seth test whether the gingerbread men were ready to eat?

p.11 (HaT) Why did the gingerbread man run away?

p.12 (FF) Who else started running after the gingerbread man?

p.13 (FF) Why did they stop to rest?

p.14 (FF) Who did the gingerbread man meet?

p.15 (HaT) Why did the crafty old fox lick his lips?

Questions to read and answer

(Children complete without your help.)

1. Seth got the gingerbread men out of the oven at
   eleven o'clock / six o'clock / seven o'clock.

2. Seth bit off the gingerbread man's **head / leg**.

3. Seth and Ann yelled **go / stop / hello**.

4. The fox led him to his **box / den / oven**.

5. The fox licked his **legs / head / lips**.

Speedy Green Words

Ask children to practise reading the words across the rows, down the columns and in and out of order clearly and quickly.

pushed	head	bread	spread
bottom	bread	head	catch
singing	kitchen	last	think
left	next	jumped	began
rest	help	running	thanks